CLOT
AND COST

written by David Alderton *and* Dawn Stubbs
illustrated by Studio Boni/Galante

CONTENTS

WHY DO PEOPLE WEAR CLOTHES?

People first started to wear clothes to keep themselves warm. During the ice age in Europe, about 30,000 years ago, people wore skins of the animals which they had hunted. In hot climates, people used clothes mainly for decoration.

Papua New Guinea
The Papuans, who live in the Highlands of Papua New Guinea, use cloth made from the bark of local trees for material to make their clothes. Birds of paradise feathers, and those of other colourful birds, are used to make headdresses.

North America
North American Indians used to wear leggings made from the skin of bison or deer. Birds' feathers were used to decorate Indian head-dresses and they wore brightly coloured leather shoes, called moccasins, which provided protection from sharp stones and the spines of cacti.

Lapland
Living in a cold northern part of the world, Laplanders rely on their clothes for warmth. They wear boots made of reindeer hide, and reindeer hair mittens. The colourful hat worn by a man is called the 'cap of four winds'. If all the points face forwards, this shows that he is unmarried.

EARLY CLOTHES AND CIVILISATIONS

Since the dawn of time, different cultures have had their own styles of dress. This often relates to the way that people live. Rare and costly materials such as silk were used to make the clothes of wealthy people, while ordinary people wore much more basic clothing. Changes in fashion still took place even thousands of years ago as lifestyles altered.

Greeks

An early Greek would have worn a **peplos**, which was held in place over the shoulders with special pins. But after a soldier was stabbed to death by these dagger-like pins, the **chiton** came into fashion. This was tied over the shoulders, and round the waist, with the lower part then resembling a skirt.

Romans

Although Romans wore a basic tunic, it was the **toga** that showed that they were citizens of Rome. Togas had a simple design, using a length of material that was draped over the shoulder. By the end of the Roman Empire, togas were used mainly for ceremonial purposes. Important officials could be recognised by the purple bands on their togas.

Celts and Vikings

In northern Europe people needed warm clothes. The men usually wore woollen trousers and a shirt, with an outer tunic that was held in place by a belt. The women had long tunics and woollen stockings. Metal jewellery, especially armlets, were popular, while antlers and bones were carved into hair combs.

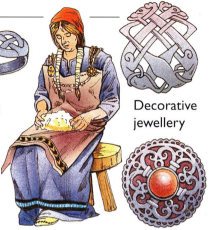

Decorative jewellery

Egyptians

Flax, the plant used to make linen, has been grown in Egypt for thousands of years. The ancient Pharaohs, who ruled the country, and members of their court, would have worn simple linen clothes. Linen helped people to stay cool in this hot climate. Reeds were woven into shoes.

Aztecs

Aztecs used cotton for much of their clothing, and they sometimes made quilted garments. Richer Aztecs had their clothes decorated with gold and fur, as well as the magnificent tail feathers of the quetzal, a bird which was very important in their culture.

7

WESTERNISED EUROPEAN CLOTHES

As more people have started to travel to different countries, so basic clothes have become increasingly international. Hard wearing, comfortable and often colourful clothes are now popular for everyday wear.

Jeans

These are trousers made from **jean**, a very strong cotton-based fabric. It was first used for clothing over five hundred years ago. Jeans were popularised by a gold prospector, in California, America, who realised that jean was an ideal material for the tough clothes needed by gold prospectors and cowboys. The traditional colour for jeans is blue. The word 'jean' is thought to come from the old Italian name for the city of Genoa, which was Janus. This was one of the earliest centres where jean was made.

Denim

This is named after a fabric called *serge de Nîmes*, which was originally produced in the Nîmes area of southern France. **Denim** has become a classic material and is worn worldwide.

Typical western
wedding dress

Classic suits

For business meetings and formal
occasions, men and women wear
suits. The first suits for men
were made in France in the
1700s. They consisted of
breeches, a waistcoat and a top
coat. Women's suits only became
fashionable in the 1880s. After
the Second World War, women
began to wear trousers, rather
than skirts, as part of a suit.

Wedding dress

Yellow was a popular colour for
wedding dresses in Roman times.
White became popular only
during the last century. A
traditional wedding outfit has
a veil covering the face, and a
train. The bridegroom may wear
a long coat with tails behind,
grey striped trousers, and a
top hat.

MIDDLE EASTERN CLOTHES

The religion in this area is predominantly Muslim. It is traditional for a Muslim woman to wear a long cotton dress which covers her body from head to toe, with just a tiny slit for her eyes. Young girls up to the age of nine do not have to hide their faces in this way.

Turkish veils
Turkish women wear a long, narrow veil made of muslin, called a yasmak. Even their eyes are covered by a mask of thin, meshed material.

Iranian veils
The idea of women covering their bodies with cloaks and veils became widespread in the 700s. Iranian women cover their bodies with cloaks. This simple style of cloak, called a **chadri**, is made of black cotton. The cloak is wrapped round the body, and hand held in place. This creates a veil which even covers part of a woman's face.

Saudi Arabian veils
Materials used to make veils, range from cotton to muslin and silk. The extent to which the veil covers a woman's face varies in different countries.

Turbans

Men wear turbans in the Middle East, Turkey and India. Turbans are a sign of the Muslim faith. Turbans are made using a long, single piece of material, which is wrapped round the head.

Coats

In parts of the Middle East, like Afghanistan, it can be very cold, especially during the winter in mountainous areas. Men and women wear long woollen coats called chupans. These are normally white, and can either be wrapped round the body like a cloak, or worn over other clothes to keep warm.

Kilims

In Turkey and western Asia, men traditionally make rugs called 'kilims'. Often the men wear their kilims.

Women in Turkmenistan

The women in Turkmenistan, near the Middle East, wear plenty of silver jewellery – traditional gifts from their husbands. The women wear bracelets and interlinked rings, ajangle with bells, on special occasions. Silver brooches are also popular items. In this part of the world both left and right shoes are the same shape, which means that you can put them on either foot.

AFRICAN CLOTHES

The climate in Africa is mostly hot and dry, and so loose, free-flowing robes help to keep people cool. Wearing coverings on their heads protects people against sunstroke in the fierce heat of the African desert.

The Bedouin people

Many people in North Africa are **nomadic**, moving from place to place. Married women wear garments with red embroidery, often having silver coins attached to a band round their veils. Younger girls have costumes decorated with blue stitchwork.

Protective clothing

Men often wear large cloaks which may be made from camel hair. They also wear colourful head cloths which are kept in place by two thick black coils of wool. Their headdresses may hang down over their cloaks, but can also be folded up round their heads, to keep sand out of their faces during a sand storm.

The Tuareg people, who live in the Sahara desert area of Africa, are unusual because it is the men who wear a veil. The distinctive blue cotton veil, called a tagilmus, measures three metres in length when it is unravelled. The tagilmus covers a man's whole head and face, with just a small slit for his eyes. When Tuareg men eat, they have to lift up the lower part of their veils.

The colour blue
Tuareg people usually dress in blue because they believe that this colour keeps insects away. The dye used to colour their cotton clothes blue sometimes comes out of their clothes, and may stain their skin.

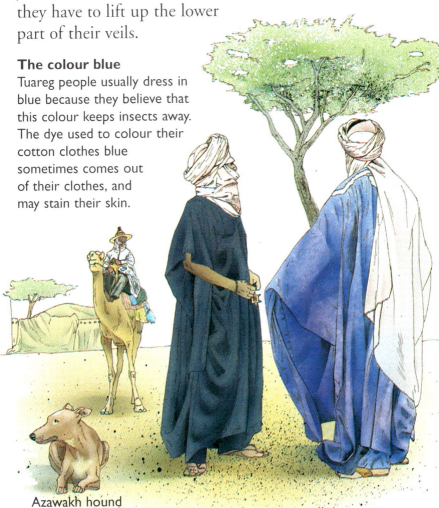

Azawakh hound

INDIAN AND SOUTHEAST ASIAN CLOTHES

Indian women drape a long piece of material, a **sari**, round their bodies. This style of dress is influenced by the **palla** of ancient Greece, and dates back to the time when the Greek ruler Alexander the Great invaded this area. The traditional shirts worn by Indian men also date back to the chiton that the Greeks wore.

Saris

Saris are made in many different styles, from various materials, including cotton, silk and nylon. A **choli** is worn under the sari with a long petticoat tied at the waist. One end of the sari, called the **pallu**, is draped over the left shoulder.

Making a sari

It takes between five and ten metres of material to make a sari. The material is usually dyed in bright colours, and may be decorated with pictures of animals and plants. A bride on her wedding day will often wear a special red sari with a green choli, complete with a long red veil draped over her head.

Punjabi suits

The younger generation of Indian girls wear Punjabi suits – trousers with a long, matching embroidered shirt.

Pallu

Choli

Batik

This method of decorating clothes has been used on Java – an island off the southeast coast of Asia – for more than 1,200 years. **Batik** is a Javanese word, which means wax painting. Hot, liquid beeswax is poured over cotton or silk.

The wax soon cools and hardens, coating the fabric. Then, when the material is dyed, the areas covered in wax cannot be reached by the dye. Beautiful patterns in the material are built up.

Special dance headdress, called a tchedah.

Distinctive jewellery worn on the fingers.

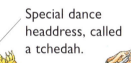

Special costume

Dance is very important in the cultures of many Asian countries. Elaborate, ornate and colourful costumes are worn for performances. In Thailand, where silk has been produced for almost 2,000 years, this material is combined with jewellery in costumes. Such costumes may be very heavy because of the precious stones sewn on to the material for decoration.

CHINESE CLOTHES

When the communists took over Chinese rule in 1949, there were attempts made to make everyone in China wear the same style of clothing, consisting of a simple blue cotton jacket and trousers. Since then, Chinese people have adopted a more individualistic style of dress, such as a silk embroidered jacket and trousers.

Symbolic dragons

Dragons have been used to decorate Chinese clothes for more than 1,000 years. The **Dragon robe**, called 'lung-p'ao', became most famous during the rule of the Ch'ing Dynasty, from 1644–1911. The colour of the robe was important; only the Emperor wore yellow.

BOUND FEET

Footbinding began in China over 1,000 years ago. From the age of six years old, girls had their toes bound back to the sole of the foot. This caused the foot to shrivel to a stump, which could then be forced into a tiny and beautiful shoe. This cruel practice went on until 1911.

JAPANESE CLOTHES

Japanese people wear **kimonos.** This garment developed from the first Japanese court costume and is based on designs worn during the Chinese T'ang dynasty 1,200 years ago. Pieces of silk, about 45 centimetres in width, are loosely sewn together. There are no buttons on a kimono. It is held in place round the waist with a sash called an **obi**, which is tied at the back.

Samurai warrior

The Samurai, who were Japanese warriors, wore special lightweight armour. The parts were laced together and weighed about 11 kilograms in total. Freedom of movement was important, and the armour hung below the waist like a skirt, divided into four pieces. The right arm was unprotected, to allow the warrior to wield his sword. Samurai also wore fearsome flared helmets on their heads.

Carved ivory hair combs.

Wooden sandals with leather straps.

17

AN ELIZABETHAN LADY

Wealthy European women and girls would have worn uncomfortable clothing during the Elizabethan period, between 1558 and 1603. The upper part of the body was held firmly in shape by a bodice. The skirt was swelled out by means of a farthingale, made from hoops of wire, wood or whalebone. The idea of a farthingale originated in Spain.

Wired collar

Ruff

Cloak

Jewelled cap

Queen Elizabeth I set a trend for red or golden wigs, which were made out of human hair or silk thread.

THE MAORIS

The Maori people arrived in New Zealand from the Polynesian islands in the Pacific Ocean about 1,000 years ago. Their clothing was simple and made from bark cloth, called tapa, which came from the paper mulberry tree. But this plant did not grow very well in New Zealand.

Maori cape

The Maoris were forced to make cloaks to protect themselves from the rain and cold in New Zealand. Woven flax was often used as a material but the most highly prized capes were made from dog skins or feathers. Special pins held these cloaks in place round the shoulders. These pins were made from pieces of shell, bone and wood, and sometimes the teeth of sperm whales.

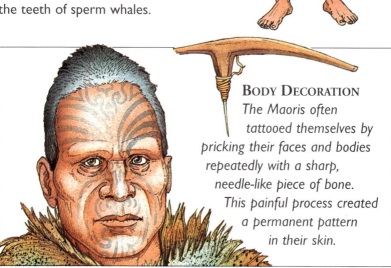

BODY DECORATION

The Maoris often tattooed themselves by pricking their faces and bodies repeatedly with a sharp, needle-like piece of bone. This painful process created a permanent pattern in their skin.

NORTH AMERICAN CLOTHES

The first people who settled in North America crossed from Asia, when these two continents were joined together, about 25,000 years ago. The native Amerindian people were often called 'Red Skins' by Europeans. This was because some Amerindians painted their bodies with red pigments. They also used body paints to decorate themselves.

Eagle feather headdress

Animal skins

Amerindians made their clothes out of animal skins. The skins were dyed red and tied together, using animal ligaments for thread.

Hunting for clothes

A wide range of animals were hunted by the Indians for their hides and fur, ranging from deer and beaver to bear and fox. The sharp quills of porcupines were also greatly valued for decorative purposes. Porcupine quills were chewed to soften them, and then dyed in various colours and used for accessory decoration.

Tipi made of buffalo hide.

The Inuit

In the far north of the American continent, the weather is harsh. The Inuit people who settled here relied on clothes made of fur to keep them warm. The women made the garments – like hooded tunics and mittens – for all the family. They used sealskin for boots, because of its waterproof qualities.

Stetson

Working cowboys

Being outside for much of the day, in the heat, cowboys wear broad rimmed felt hats, called stetsons, to keep the Sun out of their eyes. Cowboys use neck scarves, tied round their faces, for protection in a dust storm. They often wear colourful shirts and leather waistcoats and denim jeans. For extra protection, in areas of scrub where there are plants with sharp spines, cowboys have leather coverings, called **chaps**, protecting their legs.

Chaps

Tough leather boots often worn with spurs.

SOUTH AMERICAN CLOTHES

Many of the costumes from this part of the world are colourful. The Guatemalan people of Central America use natural dyes such as cochineal, from beetles, to colour their clothes. This precious dye is still exported to Europe. When mixed with tin, cochineal gives clothes a brilliant scarlet colour, or red if used on its own.

Peruvian clothes

In parts of Peru, South America, women often wear black skirts. This tradition began as a means of mourning the death of Tupac Amaru I, the last of their Inca rulers who was killed by the Spanish in 1541. Their black skirts are often decorated with a colourful border along the hem.

Keeping warm

Peruvian men often wear black trousers which may be full-length or reach just below their knees. To keep warm, they wrap brightly coloured cloaks or **ponchos** round themselves.

Simple leather sandals, held in place with a strap.

Gauchos

In southern South America, there are large areas of grassland which have been used for grazing cattle. The design of clothing here is strongly influenced by the need to ride horses. The cowboys in this part of the world are called **gauchos**. In Argentina, the men wear baggy trousers, known as **bombachas**, which can be tucked into boots.

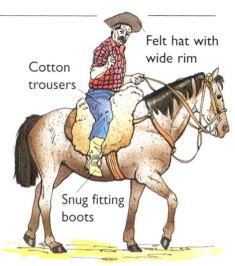

Felt hat with wide rim

Cotton trousers

Snug fitting boots

Rain forest people

It is hot and humid in rain forests and the people decorate their bodies, rather than wearing many clothes. Body paints are made using a variety of materials, including soil and plants. Bright colours are most popular. Rain forest people also use feathers and leaves to make headdresses.

South American hats

Llama and alpaca wool is often used to make distinctive brown or black hats. These hats give protection against the cold. If a woman decorates her hat with flowers, it means that she is looking for a man to marry. Rounded bowler hat styles are popular in this part of the world.

NATURAL MATERIALS

People have always used whatever materials are available in the areas where they have lived from both the animal and plant world, to make their clothes. Animal hides have been made into leather, and other materials, ranging from grasses to wool and silk, have been used to make clothes since time immemorial.

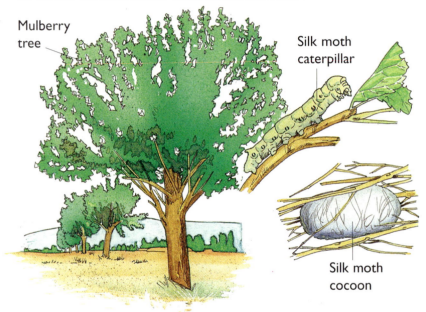

Mulberry tree

Silk moth caterpillar

Silk moth cocoon

Silk clothes

Silk fabric is produced by the caterpillar of the silk moth, as it spins its cocoon. The silk is formed in a continuous thread, which can be over 1,000 metres long. The Chinese discovered how to obtain silk over 8,000 years ago, rearing the silkworms in orchards of mulberry trees. They kept their discovery a closely-guarded secret.

But, in AD 550, two Persian monks smuggled some silk moth eggs out of China and sold them to the Roman Emperor Justinian, along with details of how silk was made. The silkworm's cocoon has to be unravelled first, and then the thread can be spun into a yarn which can be woven into silk fabric. Silk is used to make a range of clothes.

Merino sheep

Wool from sheep

Sheep are the most important source of wool. The main breed of sheep kept for the quality of its wool is the merino. The wool is removed by shearing the fleece with special clippers.

Special wools

Goats like the angora and cashmere are highly valued for their wool. In South America, llamas and alpacas provide very fine, soft wool.

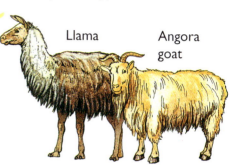

Llama

Angora goat

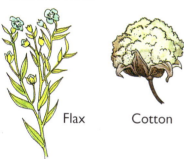

Flax   Cotton

Fabric from plants

Cotton is spun from the soft white fibres that protect the seeds of the cotton plant when the seedheads ripen. Dried fibres of the flax plant are spun and woven into linen.

Chinchilla

HUNTED FOR FASHION

The chinchilla was almost hunted to extinction for its fur. It has a very dense, soft coat to protect it from the cold in the mountains of South America where it lives. More recently, rather than hunting reptiles like lizards, snakes and crocodiles for their skins to make clothes and handbags, some of these animals have been bred on farms.

Monitor lizard

SYNTHETIC MATERIALS

Synthetic materials for clothes are made using chemicals rather than natural products like cotton. The first attempts to make artificial fabrics began in 1664, but it was not until 1884 that a recipe for artificial fabric was invented, by a Frenchman called Comte Hilaire de Chardonnet. The new material was called rayon, and was an artificial form of silk.

Nylon
The American DuPont company developed nylon from coal in 1939. This artificial fabric was first used to make stockings.

Polyester
The DuPont company later introduced a lighter fabric called polyester.

Acrylic
By the 1950s acrylic was developed and mixed with natural fibres, like wool, to make it warm and light.

Elastic
Latex, the sap from rubber trees, was first used to make rubber boots. Scientists at the DuPont company improved latex to make stretchy, elasticised clothes.

Polyester coat

Acrylic sweater

Nylon stockings

LYCRA*
This fabric is used for casual and sportswear. It stretches without splitting and is very comfortable.

LYCRA* sportswear

*DuPont's registered trademark.

SPECIAL CLOTHES

Innovative synthetic materials have helped people to design clothes for particular purposes. Fabrics with specific properties have been used for hi-tech, specialised and comfortable sportswear.

Keeping dry and warm

When you exercise, your body produces heat and you become warmer. If this heat remains trapped below layers of clothing, you will sweat heavily and soon feel uncomfortable. A fabric called ® GORE-TEX is waterproof and also allows moist air out.

Rain and wind cannot penetrate inwards.

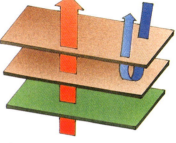

Cross section of ® GORE-TEX fabric.

Body moisture can escape outwards.

Breathable clothes

The ® GORE-TEX fabric is made of layers of water resistant nylon and polyester with one-and-a-half billion tiny pores per square centimetre of material. This allows your body heat and moisture out but does not allow rain in.

Velcro

Pieces of Velcro are often used as fasteners instead of buckles or shoe laces. Velcro sticks together and can be pulled apart repeatedly.

® GORE-TEX is a registered mark of W L Gore and Associates Inc.

DESIGNING CLOTHES

The fashion industry began by producing clothes mainly for individual people. Today, the results of the work of fashion designers are on sale in clothes' shops in many different countries. Designers often use computers to help to provide a clear picture of what their new designs will look like, when finished. This can also help them to work out how much material will be required, and even the likely cost of the finished garment.

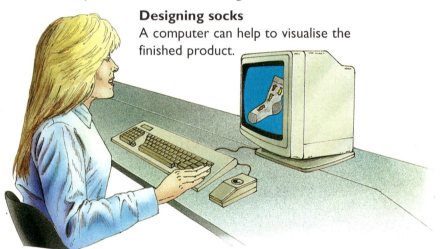

Designing socks
A computer can help to visualise the finished product.

Computer aided design
Computers help fashion designers to portray their ideas. For example, a computer can redraw and repeat a pattern many times, in seconds, saving hours of repetitive drawing. Also, a designer can visualise different colour combinations, simply with one keystroke. By making changes in this way, the whole design process becomes much quicker.

A fashion show
Designers display their new collections of clothes at fashion shows. Models walk down a catwalk, raised off the ground, so that everyone can see the new garments.

Individualistic styles
Fashion designers often adopt distinctive styles.

AMAZING CLOTHES & COSTUME FACTS

- **Invisible suit** A special suit has been invented which makes you invisible. The incredible outfit is covered with thousands of fibre optic wires. These carry light from one side of your body and make it come out on the other side. The effect means that people can see straight through you.

- **Stitching up** Thimbles were first used in Roman times to protect the thumb or finger whilst sewing. They were often made of leather.

- **The origin of the anorak** In the winter, the Inuit of North America wear two hooded tunics one on top of the other. This gives them a layer of fur next to their bodies, and another outside to protect them from the cold. This type of snug clothing is called an 'anorak' in Greenland, and a 'parka' in the Aleutian Islands, off the northeast coast of Asia.

- **Battle clothing** The woollen head covering known as a 'balaclava' is named after the port near the Black Sea which was occupied by the British army during the Crimean War of 1853-1856. Balaclavas give good protection against the cold and hide people's faces.

- **Appearance of pockets** Women's clothes did not have pockets until the 19th century, and so hanging purses were used instead.

- **Masses of materials** In the 1850s, the crinoline was introduced. This cage of hoops, which hung underneath dresses, often needed more than 40 metres of material to fit over it.

GLOSSARY

Batik An Asian method of painting fabric with wax, to prevent the waxed part of the fabric taking up a dye. This creates patterns on the fabric.

Bombachas Baggy trousers, worn by gauchos in Argentina, South America.

Breeches Knee length trousers that used to be worn by men.

Chadri A garment that covers the entire body from head to toe. It is usually worn by women of the Muslim faith.

Chaps Protective leather covering worn over jeans by cowboys.

Chiton A tunic worn by men and women in ancient Greece.

Choli This garment is worn on the upper part of the body, like a blouse, beneath a sari, and it is usually patterned.

Denim A fabric which was first made in southern France, and is now used to make jeans.

Dragon robe Decorated by dragons, this robe became part of the official dress in China during the rule of the Ch'ing dynasty.

Gaucho A cowboy in Argentina, South America.

Jean Tough cotton material used to make jeans.

Kimono A long, traditional Japanese garment, with no buttons and wide sleeves.

Nomadic People who do not live in a particular place, but who travel through a region, stopping for water and food.

Obi The sash worn with a kimono.

Palla A kind of cloak worn by women, which can be draped over the head or shoulders.

Pallu The part of a sari which covers the left shoulder.

Peplos A loose tunic worn by women in ancient Greece.

Poncho The type of cloak worn in South America that can also be used as a blanket.

Sari The long, flowing garment worn by Indian women.

Toga The formal garment, usually made from wool, worn by men in ancient Rome.

INDEX *(Entries in **bold** refer to an illustration)*